'As each breaker retreated,
the shoreline broke
into an ever-widening grin.'

John Fante, *Ask the Dust*

particles of wonder

everywhere they looked

the kids
saw
particles of wonder

tiny
golden
turd-shaped
puffs of magic
dancing before
giggling eyes

the adults
too busy with their own shit

the impossible menu

I walked through the restaurant
sat down
and asked for the menu

'would you like
The Possible
or
The Impossible
Menu
Sir?'
asked the maître d'

curious
I asked for the
impossible

clicking his fingers
a waiter appeared
dragging a menu
constructed from clouds

for my starter I chose
Carpaccio of Cold Water Mermaid
drizzled in a Unicorn jus
delicious!

for mains my selection was
two large baked Ghost Whales
stuffed with Moon-Cactus mash
in a White Stag sauce
unbelievable!

whilst for dessert I chose
shavings of a deliciously creamy
young goat-god
resting on mountains of ice-cream from
    the centre of the sun
topped with a Hobgoblin glaze
garnished
with fresh Mars crumbs
and a curl of crispy cosmic coulis

outta this world!

needless to say
when the establishment was raided
I was so gorged
I couldn't
even walk
to the police van

so instead they carried me
like a giant larva fit to burst

lucky for me
my lawyer noted that I couldn't be held responsible
for
ordering the
impossible

the mountain of eternal orgasm

was a difficult
but rewarding
climb

he created weather around him

wherever he went
he created weather
around
him

at home
fog seeped through the carpets
in the post-office
it started to rain
in the newsagents
lightning struck the shelves
at the carwash
it snowed
in the library
thunder clapped
and
at the bank
an electrical storm
failed
to unlock the safe

but in prison
he
eventually
got the knack of it
the sun
blasting
a man-sized hole in the wall of his cell
as he flew
off
on a fast-moving cloud

her own private aurora borealis

she had always
had her
own
private aurora borealis

from the moment
of her birth
the northern lights
danced
around her

exhaling
and
inhaling
with her
every
breath

solar winds singing
in adulation

the villagers
tutting
at the strange
newcomer

but at least
she saved them
on
street lighting

the aromatic agnostic

the aromatic agnostic
took her place
with all the other hopefuls
in the church

the worshippers' heads turning
in search
of
the wonderful scent
that had appeared in their midst

even the man in flowing robes
at the altar
stopped his incantations
hunting
for the fragrance
making all giddy
with delight

the aromatic agnostic
had not expected this
having decided
on a whim
to see
what
all
the god fuss was about

shoulders lowered
eyes gazing at her feet
she tried to shrink
to become

invisible

but it was no use
soon she was sniffed out

surrounded by
the good folks
pressing up against her skin
inhaling her scent
arms reaching out to touch her
people crying out in desperation
just to be near her
she found herself
sympathising
with deities throughout the centuries

Odin, Thor, Apollo, Dagda, Amida, Kane, Awha, Freya,
Jarilo, Nezha, Ganesha, Shiva, Hanuman,
Allah, Chango, Obatala
and God
all came before her to offer advice
suggesting patience
and thick skin
to be necessary traits
to shoulder the burden of belief

celestial entities of wisdom and thunder
cavorting with divinities of music and dance

spirits of beginnings
backslapping
supreme beings of procreation

demons of war demanding duels with everyone

all trembling
before
the All Powerful All Knowing Ruler
of the Universe and the Creator
of Everything in Existence

many of the gathered idols
who'd lost their allure
over the centuries
begging
for early retirement
when they could
at last
go on an almighty
everlasting
bender

the aromatic agnostic now realising
that
although
she was no longer
agnostic
she sure as hell
was still
aromatic
as
the people
nibbled away
at

all

that
she had to offer

the orchestra to his orgasm

no matter where he was
every time he had sex
an
ORCHESTRA
appeared

the conductor madly waving his baton
as they built to the dramatic climax

losing him many girlfriends

until
he met someone
with a sense
of
occasion

nobody had told him

nobody had told him
he was different
until he turned eighteen
but at his party

surprisingly

as his dad
unzipped his skin
whilst
his mother's hair
morphed
into dancing tentacles
and
his older brother
flashed
an explosive grin
of such atomic
brilliance
that
without the seven layers of indestructible film
over his
increasingly
oval eyes
the birthday boy would have been blinded
forever

he was unsurprised

having always thought
his family
was from another planet

you had such potential

'you had such potential'

sighed

his demanding mother
just before
the musician
received
his
Godlike Genius
award

the professor of plagiarism

the professor of plagiarism
entered the university quiz
competing in the final
against the Ethics Department

his answers
an exact match
to those of his opponents

and was soon
copied

into his dismissal notice

the lonely photofit

the lonely photofit
joined a dating app
rearranging his features
for each potential match

doing nothing to help his chances
of ever finding
a
perfect
fit

the omelette in a fluffy bathrobe

the omelette in a fluffy bathrobe
had enjoyed staying at the hotel

luxuriating in the power shower
swigging from the minibar
pocketing tiny soap bars
and
watching TV
whilst spread out on a king-size bed

but decided to skip
breakfast

raining solar-powered ice-cold beer-fridges in the desert

it was raining solar-powered ice-cold beer-fridges
in the desert
when the nomads arrived

deciding
to call it home

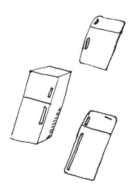

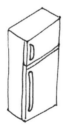

I saw a man today

I saw a man
today
in the changing rooms
at the swimming pool

a very small man
a skinny man
with a large stomach

an impossible-to-age man

with legs
so thin
they could snap
just by
looking at them

he was wearing beige trunks

they stuck to him like someone else's skin

he could have been a baby

or an old man
or something in-between

he trod carefully over the tiles
slowly
lifting his knees high

an old-stork-man-baby
wading
backwards and forwards
through his life

and dried himself off
with a towel
that had seen better days

I want to see a picture of that man's anus before lunchtime

*I want to see a picture of that man's
    anus before lunchtime*
he barked

passers-by
glad
he
was
a surgeon

money sounds like

to the billionaire
money sounds like
the gentle splash of perfect waves against
    a perfect yacht
the cushioned thud of a private-jet landing
    on a private island
the hummingbird flutter of silk underwear
    floating onto a $4.5m Persian rug
and
the roar of rocket engines as the space-tourist
    space-craft hurtles towards Mars

whilst to the poor
money sounds like
another
world

so many near misses

in this city
every second
someone
has a close call with death

a bus's wing mirror
narrowly misses
the head
of a pedestrian

a mighty truck's
mighty tyres
pass
an inch away
from a stilettoed foot

a child
teeters
on the edge
of a curb

a cat crosses
a busy street

and an old lady
doesn't see
the motorbike
coming

the grim reaper
wearing a high vis jacket
waiting

patiently

on every
street corner

our children play with empty bullet-cases

our children play with empty bullet-cases
said the fighter
as war-planes

circled above

promising
bigger toys

the cladding of indifference

they added
the cladding of indifference
to the tower blocks
of the poor
to give the billionaires
a better view

cheap pastel shades
customising poverty
destroying stains

got tenants to fill in Health & Safety forms
replacing sprinklers
with
dotted lines
to be signed...

and
then

when the fire took hold

the cold-blooded cladding
of not-caring
didn't give a damn
mocking
newborn and old cries
alike

the disdain of indifference
the brutality of apathy
hidden behind
a smokescreen
of legality

the cheapest cladding of indifference
banned abroad
dark number-crunching hearts
making a killing

and after
the building
stood
smouldering
they did
so

little

to comfort
feed
and
house
the
grief-stricken
bedraggled
and
traumatised

instead

they
came
briefly

surrounded by a phalanx
of security
to dip their toes into
another reality

pulling back in distaste to their
chauffeur-driven
perfectly-cladded
custom-built
fire-proofed
Jaguar cars

the
depravity
of austerity
rearing its head

the fire
igniting
a fury
that can never
be put out

*Dedicated to the victims of the Grenfell Tower
fire and those who continue to fight for justice.*

the caring algorithm

lied

I can't imagine the world without me

one evening
I was standing
at the bar
and blurted out
how I couldn't imagine
the world
without me

at which
everyone
raised their drinks
and shouted
me too

pandemic poem #1

part I

the dread
the ensuing dread
the thing to come

the thing
the certain uncertainty

driving us crazy
this virus

arriving
unseen

its effects
more than
visible

but maybe not!

maybe
our leaders have it under control!

as the wealthy
buy ventilators
and the poor
buy toilet roll

but we've watched it
coming our way
twiddling our thumbs

not getting it
this 'other people' thing
it couldn't happen to *us*

we're not like *them*

part II

children playing next door
the coo of pigeons
a breeze through trees
the echo of trains
footsteps on empty pavements
the moan of a dog barking
the clanking grind of a dustbin truck
a little blast of music from an upstairs flat
the screech of cat sex
the clink of neighbours' plates
a wailing saxophone through an open window
the thud of a solitary football
muffled voices
the crank of heating systems coming on
the buzz of insects
&
the urgency
of
approaching sirens

part III

two young sisters took the cat out
on a leash

cos they'd heard
you could
go out for a walk
with a pet

no way
was it going to obey

part IV

the woman in self-isolation
looked out of her window

not a plane in sight

but she did spot
a white-tailed eagle
souring through the shadows
of past vapour trails
it's broad wings with fingered ends
fluttering in the breeze
as she waved back

delighting
in
empty skies

a glass of clarity

a glass of

clarity

goes
a long way
in
a

    c
o
            n
      f

u   s
          e

              d

      world

you know you're in love when your reality is better than your dreams

which was a shame
as when he woke up

the troupe of Las Vegas showgirls

had
vanished
from
his
bedsit

take her to the special place

take her to the special place
were his sex guru's
words
so he bought two first class plane tickets
packed the holiday bags
and opened
their bedroom door

only
to discover
she'd already
reached Paradise

with
Bob

I looked for you at the whorehouse

'I looked for you at the whorehouse'
said the gambler
to the priest
during confession

knowing it was not
such
a long
shot

one day he would hand her
a pistol and tell her the truth

one day he would hand her a pistol and tell her the truth
but
until then
he'd lie

we are all statistics

'we are all statistics'
noted the statistician
as he stood on the beach
explaining

to the gathered children

that his cells
would stretch to the sun and back
61 times

and his
10 pints of blood
would be enough
to feed
100 vampire bats
for
20 days

and his
32 teeth
if made into an axe
would be able to chop through
13 feet of silver birch wood
before they broke

and he would
of course
have been able to work out
the chances of becoming
the first
collector and interpreter of numerical data
to be killed
by a suicidal seagull

if only
he had known

undressed by the air

undressed
by the air
she fell to earth

staring
in slow-motion disbelief
as a man
clad only in his socks

hurtled
past her

along with another
still strapped into his chair

a
child
plummeting
through the clouds

with the words
'don't panic'
emblazoned across
his flapping t-shirt

the sky raining humans

but it was
the couple embracing
in mid-air
that took
her breath
away

before she landed
naked and dead

in a stranger's kitchen
surrounded
by fields of ripening sunflowers
she would
never
see

Dedicated to the victims of Flight
MH17 shot down over Ukraine.

you can't plan an epiphany

'you can't plan an epiphany'
sighed
the crestfallen pilgrim
who'd tried everything

crawled on bleeding knees up holy Irish
    slate mountains
cried out for his Father as he was crucified
    under a hot Filipino sun
chanted Sanskrit whilst living naked on top
    of an Indian wooden pole
flagellated himself with razor-sharp Iranian chains

not forgetting

when he was chosen to be the Naked Man
    at the Japanese Shinto festival
where he'd had all his body-hair shaved
    and then ran through the streets
pursued by thousands of emotional
    Sake-drenched devotees
in their scramble to touch him for good luck

all to no avail

no flash of understanding
no bolt of revelation
nothing...

so, while in Japan
he decided to undertake the ultimate test of
self-mummification

surviving on bark and poisonous tea
he exercised continually for three years
jettisoning all fat and fluid from his body
leading
to
The Big Day
when he sealed himself inside a stone tomb
so small
he could
only
move his mouth

breathing through an air tube attached
to a bell
the
only
sign
he was still alive

the day the ringing stopped
the gathered monks pulled the tube free
closing the tomb forever

none the wiser

as to whether
this
pilgrim

had found
what
he was looking for

the last selfie

all around the world
people are
getting hit by trains
falling off cliffs
crashing planes
and
shooting themselves
in the head
whilst taking
that last
selfie...

distraught relatives
tenderly placing their beloved's final
frozen moment
upon
the
coffin
as they take turns
to snap away

before
tripping over
backwards
into
the
grave

whilst we value your death

when he approached
The Pearly Gates
he found himself
in
a
queue

a voice explaining

whilst we value your death
we are currently experiencing an unusually
     high volume of traffic
current waiting time:

eternity

never cross the great magnet

'NEVER cross the great magnet'
warned the small-town cop

thinking he was sun-stroked
or just plain crazy
I ignored the fucker

driving across the desert
not another living being in sight
I noticed how
the car
was speeding up

pumping the brake
taking my hands off the wheel
and burning holes in the tyres
with my cigar
making no goddam difference

the machine flying straight as a bullet

in the distance I saw
a large dark object
hovering over hazy sun-bleached terrain

the closer I came to the thing
the more the cop's words
came back to haunt me
as it was indeed
a fuckin' great magnet
hovering over the earth
its very core
sucking me onwards
drawing me towards
its metallic self

the more I looked at it
the more captivating it became
and I wondered
about its
hypnotic power

it was now
only a few miles away
and I was staggered
by its size

larger than a baseball stadium
larger than the alimony I had to pay out
    to my ex-wives every month
larger than the pink elephant I'd ridden
    at the grand opening of The Bellagio casino
larger than all the shattered dreams
    of the gamblers I'd ever met

onwards it pulled me

I tried to throw myself out of the car
but found myself driven back into my seat
by the force that was dragging me
kicking and screaming
towards
certain oblivion

then an idea!
its a fuckin' magnet

and threw off my
watch
shades
neck chain

what else?

of course - my belt buckle

so to be sure
I stripped off
completely
leaving me
staring at
that goddam
metal
stud and ring
in the end of my cock

holy shit!

just as I was hunched over
yanking at the ring
I heard
the siren
of that patrol car
and turned to see
the hick cop
bearing down on me
lights flashing
a knight of the road
come to my rescue!

but instead he sped by
in an inbred blur of shades and stubble
and parked up ahead of me
as I noticed for the first time
that his car
was made of rubber

taking out a
plastic camera
he took pictures
as I flew past
naked
and
bloody

even through his shades
I knew that look

the
I told you so
look
of a small town cop

holy holy shit!

I'd always known
my cock
would get me
into trouble

but not like this

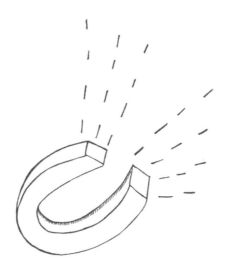

noodle dress

the noodle dress
slipped off
with
a slurp

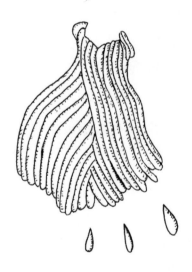

the collective-noun collector

the collective-noun collector's
first collection
proved to be a clever move

a shrewdness of apes
announcing him as one to watch

his follow-up
a business of ferrets
attracting investors
but
he screwed up
with a crash of rhinoceroses
escaping from his warehouse
causing highway havoc and endless lawsuits

an unkindness of ravens
laughing
at yet more
misfortune to come...

a parcel of perfectly wrapped penguins
going missing in the post

a plague of locusts
doing exactly what it said
on the tin

adding injury to insult
whilst chasing
a rabble of butterflies
he tripped over a nuisance of cats
breaking his leg in three places
but
took the enforced time-out to plot a better future
captivating
the market upon his return
with a charm
of
hummingbirds

cash cascading
into
his
coffers

leading to a big celebration with a party of jays
lasting for days
a rhumba of rattlesnakes
taking to the stage
with a quiver
of backing-singing cobras
before
the headlining band of coyotes
trashed the place

a mischief of mice hitting the DJ decks
causing an unlikely fight
between
an implausibility of gnus and a smack of jellyfish
the knot of frogs
complicating matters no end

and once all
the booze
and
drugs
had been devoured
and all kinds
of DISGUSTING
interspecies sex had occurred
the collector went ballistic
discovering his money

guarded

by a sword of mallards
had vanished
along with the mallards

followed shortly
by a knock on the door
from the police
investigating
a murder of crows

and decided to start collecting art

the drifting bird

the tv crew
trained its cameras
on the beautiful bird
as it drifted by
on a bed
of floating water weeds

then later
it rode past
on the back
of a swamp rat

until at sunset
it passed by
for the last time

on the snout
of an alligator

even a Komodo Dragon's
bite couldn't slow him down

'even a Komodo Dragon's bite couldn't slow him down'
said
the impressed
Komodo Dragon

shaking hands with a monkey
is like going back in time

thought the hardworking zookeeper
as
the oldest

most

leathery
hand in
the world

reached out

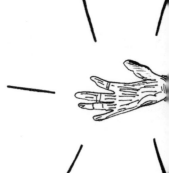

and clasped his
fingers tight

ancient connections
zapping him
through
the jungle
of
ancestors
to
an age

when they had both
been free

the pretty fly

the pretty fly
was

pretty fly

it's not rocket science

'it's not rocket science'
she sighed
as her husband
struggled
to open
a tin of beans

before heading
off
to her job
as a
rocket scientist

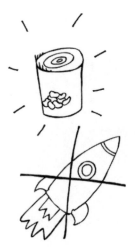

kimchi kimono

in the restaurant
at the top
of the Gherkin building

the cocktail waitress's
Kimchi Kimono
fell open

the married man
finding himself
in a pickle

breaking up

apparently, we're breaking up
he said to his wife
whilst listening
down
a
bad
phone
line

to their
therapist

it's not that I don't love you

'it's not that I don't love
you
but I love
Bali
more'

said
his wife
with
the sun
and beach
behind her
a thousand miles away
from where he sat hunched up
in their cold home

nodding
in understanding
he slammed
the laptop shut
with
a
bang

hot-footing it
to
the airport

hurricane memories

a few months after the hurricane
the lover
walked through
a sea
of
people
at
the lost photograph warehouse

so many eyes
searching
for
those memories

the ones
that were
washed away
in a
torrent
   of
        wind
water
                    and debris

their lives
now incomplete

frag
   me
nt
         ed

a jigsaw
puzzle   with
        missing
    p   e   c   e   s

that birthday party
that holiday

and
those faces

now

                                        swept away

just like her

rain bloody rain

it poured
and poured
bloody rains
from the heavens

I saw the sky open up a vein

a suicidal god
unable to die?

a junkie god
going awry?

I have no real idea

but now and then
I give
a nod
to the
Most High

sodium city

I've been traveling
since
I can remember

looking for extraordinary places
and
extraordinary people
but
nothing
had prepared me
for the
sodium city
floating
high
above the mountains

at first
I thought it was a mirage
but an unattached lift
zipped
me up
to The Grand Entrance
where a chemist
asked
endless questions
and took away
my water
explaining
that sodium and H2O
are not a good mix

(I thought of my last marriage
and nodded in understanding of such things)

let through the barricades
I leaned against a silver-white wall
and found myself
slipping
into the sodium
until I was trapped

a man in a crisp white uniform
cut me out with a butter knife
his eyes rolling
as if he'd done this a thousand times

exploring narrow backstreets
I heard a siren go off
and saw demonstrators
throwing water at buildings
protesting at the difficulty of living in such a place

where the drops hit
the sodium came alive
breaking off into pea-sized pieces
ricocheting off surfaces

sparkling diamond bullets
knocking people down
their blood bright
against the silver city

I stared at the sky
looking for an answer
noticing
for the first time
that this place existed in some kind of
transparent protective sphere
maybe to prevent rain
from turning everyday life
into a game of deadly pinball

after the mayhem had ceased
and the injured and dead taken
to the places
of the injured and dead
I found my way back to the chemist at the gate
and asked
why
anyone would build a city out of what this was made?

looking at me like I was crazy
he replied
'because it is extraordinary'

Dedicated to Sir Humphry Davy,
Cornish Chemist who discovered Sodium
and enjoyed inhaling laughing gas.

spiders on acid

the renegade scientist

proved

that spiders
made
terrible webs
on caffeine
and
beautiful ones
on acid

but that
didn't help
as
he stared out
of his prison window

until
he noticed
a huge intricate network
of
gossamer threads

inching
            its

                                    way
towards

                    him

in the shape
            of
        a
ladder

the silent applause of stars

the silent applause of stars
meant

everything

to
the brilliant
unknowns
taking bows
under
hopeful skies

24 hours to get out of town

24 hours
was never going to be enough
to get out of town

first
there were
all
the families
to hold tight
before
the young men
hit the bars
to pay their respects
to iron-fisted barkeeps with their assortment
of bleary-eyed barflies
saying adios as they went
to star-gazing stoners
cock-a-hoop pool kings
bad-luck gamblers
too-stocky-to-be-a-jockey-jockeys
grizzly down 'n outs
&
fast frenetic speed freaks
who could talk the hind legs off a donkey
if that's what was needed
to keep silence at bay

along the way

toasting
drunken 3 a.m. poets

back-slapping
muscle-bound-ex-boxer-bouncers
with no necks and tiny eyes
for whom the crowd
had once
brayed their names
as if they were gods
when they entered the ring

dancing
with louder-and-larger-than-life drag-acts
who'd overcome everything
to be who they are

singing
songs with musicians so brilliant
no one could understand why their faces
weren't on every billboard

and of course

doing deals
with the dealers
who fuelled much of the above

amidst all these farewells
the young men forgot
to check their watches
as the bullets
of the gangsters they'd offended
flew past their skulls

crowds of well-wishers
rushing
to their rescue
giving them a chance
to kiss all the girls goodbye

the young men glad
that 24 hours
was never going
to be enough
to get
out of this town

Thanks to...

R.J. Ellory and his fellowship of two fingers.

A.M. Archer, the musical tour de force behind Marlon-Q.

Cerys Matthews for falling for the possum and bringing the critter to the people.

Dave 'Daggers' Holman and his launch capability to fly and survive.

Susannah Herbert of National Poetry Day for bolstering bards everywhere.

Scott McMahon and Suzi Martin for Raising the Bar as always.

Johnny 'The Bear' Munro for The Scarborough Connection.

Vic Bastable of Harmonic Artists for Good-Life-Bonhomie.

Timotei Cole for the chapel of poems.

Richard Abbott for his instantaneous outta-this-world colour-blind-design flair.

Dr Phil Jackson and his extraordinary ringmaster panache.

Peter Barnfather for his punk graphics.

Toni Davidson, the keeper of words.

Michael Ptootch for keeping the faith.

Oli Sylvester and Dan Towler for creative camaraderie.

Stephen Jones aka Babybird for his yearning soundtracks that
sometimes insist upon joining me on stage.

Matt & gang at Hobs Repro Farringdon for their sign-print-
ing finesse.

All those who ride the wave at the Lady H.

And of course thumbs up to those outrageously wonderful
amigos too dodgy and numerous to mention (unlike last time
when ink was cheaper) and family: ProfBro, Minx and B for
constantly usurping me in the word and picture stakes, Don
Daddio for his maverick wit that led to the poem 'whilst we
value your death' and MightyMa for dancing like there is no
tomorrow. Big applause also goes out to Emily Elizabeth Talbot
for pointing out that 'you can't plan an epiphany'. And Huxley
for blowing us all away with his magic. Big Cheers to G 'n T.

Waving a huge Gonzo fist to Hunter S. Thompson for ener-
gising 'never cross the great magnet'.

And finally, hats off to Valley Press's indestructible Jamie
McGarry for shining his genius spotlight-of-attention upon
these poems and getting this book into your, fingers-crossed,
post-pandemic clean hands.

That's all folks!

— contact the poet —
mark@markwaddell.com

PARTICLES OF WONDER

More at home in a bar than a library, Mark Waddell often takes to the stage mixing cocktails of music and words. He is also the man behind the street signs that are part of London's Kentish Town landscape, keeping passers-by intrigued and tickled pink.

particles of wonder follows on from his debut collection *on the cusp of greatness* and the appearance of 'the sound of a falling possum' in *Tell Me the Truth About Life: A National Poetry Day Anthology* curated by Cerys Matthews, where he found himself sandwiched between Maya Angelou, Leonard Cohen, Sylvia Plath and William Shakespeare.

You can follow Mark's street signs on Instagram: @onthecuspofgreatness

Particles of Wonder

MARK WADDELL

Chris
keep weaving
your magic !

Mark

VP

Valley Press

First published in 2021 by Valley Press
Woodend, The Crescent, Scarborough, YO11 2PW
www.valleypressuk.com

ISBN 978-1-912436-56-9
Cat. no. VP0177

Cover and text design by Peter Barnfather.
Cover photograph by Pip Letchworth.
Edited by Jamie McGarry.

Printed and bound in the EU by Pulsio, Paris.

Contents

for...

Wabbit & Huxley
Balletic Yvonne and Peter 'The Don' Waddell
&
Lifesaver Pip Letchworth

thinking of...

Andy 'Bong & Shirley Show' McDonald
Gentle Joe Dalton
&
Peter 'Le Guillotine' Phelps